£3.50   To Chris, Katrina, Mark, Rachel
            + N

Thank you a
all the fun times we spent
together at 'No 102'
        Best of luck for 1982.

            Lots of Love
                Philippa xxx
    January 1982.

POEMS OF
BANJO PATERSON

POEMS OF
BANJO PATERSON

Illustrated by Pro Hart

LANSDOWNE PRESS
Sydney • Auckland • London • New York

Published by Lansdowne Press Sydney
176 South Creek Road, Dee Why West, NSW, Australia 2099
First published 1974
2nd Impression 1975
3rd Impression 1978
4th Impression 1979
5th Impression 1980
Poems © Grace Harvie 1974
Paintings © Copyright Pro Hart 1974
Produced in Australia by the Publisher
Typeset in Australia by Filmset Centre Pty Ltd, Brisbane
Printed in Singapore by
Kyodo-Shing Loong Press Pte Ltd

National Library of Australia Cataloguing-in-Publication Data

Paterson, Andrew Barton, 1864-1941.
  Poems of Banjo Paterson. Volume 1.

Previously published, Sydney: Ure Smith, 1974.
ISBN 0 7018 1378 4

I. Hart, Pro, 1928-, illus. II. Title.

A821'.2

The Poems

Prelude

I have gathered these stories afar
In the wind and the rain,
In the land where the cattle-camps are,
On the edge of the plain.
On the overland routes of the west,
When the watches were long,
I have fashioned in earnest and jest
These fragments of song.

They are just the rude stories one hears
In sadness and mirth,
The records of wandering years—
And scant is their worth.
Though their merits indeed are but slight,
I shall not repine
If they give you one moment's delight,
Old comrades of mine.

Introduction

As the author of the famous ballads *Clancy of the Overflow, Waltzing Matilda,* and *The Man from Snowy River,* Andrew Barton ('Banjo') Paterson, has become a symbol of the outback for most Australians. But he managed to cram into an eventful life a great deal more than just writing bush ballads. He was also lawyer, grazier, traveller, journalist, editor, war correspondent, soldier, sportsman, and noted horseman.

Paterson was born on 17th February, 1864 at Narambla, near Orange in New South Wales. During his childhood on his father's property he became an expert horseman and many of his later poems commemorate his love of horse-racing and polo.

He was educated at Sydney Grammar, and during his schooldays lived with his grandmother, Emily Barton, at Gladesville. She wrote poetry and exerted a significant influence over the young Paterson. At sixteen he matriculated and was articled to a Sydney law firm.

Paterson began writing and contributing verse to *The Bulletin* during the late 1880s. He used the pseudonym of 'The Banjo', after a racehorse his father had owned, and his work soon became very popular.

He loved the Australian outback, and combined in verse both action itself and the landscape of action. And there is always in all his writings the laconic humour and fatalistic philosophy of the bushman—constantly faced with drought, heat, flies and dust—yet never going under.

Paterson's poetry belongs to the ballad tradition, the folk poetry passed down to us from the Mediaeval bards. He took the ballad genre and moulded it to fit his songs and stories of the Australian bush. His poems capture exactly the spirit and essence of the people, the vast distances and the harsh and beautiful places of outback Australia.

Through many of his ballads he also became one of Australia's greatest myth makers, not least in *Waltzing Matilda*. His jolly swagman, written to the tune of an old English marching song, has become so symbolic of Australia that it is the nearest thing we have to an indigenous national anthem.

Banjo Paterson was a true folk poet—many of his poems are as much a part of the Australian way of life and tradition as steak and eggs, Bondi Beach and beer. In his lifetime he published several books of verse, two novels, a collection of short stories, a book of memoirs, and the first collection of Australian bush songs. But even more than that, he helped form the Australian heritage and gave city people a glimpse of the beauty and legendary magic of the bush.

Clancy of the Overflow

I HAD written him a letter which I had, for want of better
   Knowledge, sent to where I met him down the Lachlan years ago;
He was shearing when I knew him, so I sent the letter to him,
   Just on spec, addressed as follows, "Clancy, of The Overflow".

And an answer came directed in a writing unexpected
   (And I think the same was written with a thumb-nail dipped
      in tar);
'Twas his shearing mate who wrote it, and *verbatim* I will quote it:
   "Clancy's gone to Queensland droving, and we don't know where
      he are."

     .   .   .   .   .

In my wild erratic fancy visions come to me of Clancy
   Gone a-droving "down the Cooper" where the Western drovers go;
As the stock are slowly stringing, Clancy rides behind them singing,
   For the drover's life has pleasures that the townsfolk never know.

And the bush has friends to meet him, and their kindly voices
      greet him
   In the murmur of the breezes and the river on its bars,
And he sees the vision splendid of the sunlit plains extended,
   And at night the wondrous glory of the everlasting stars.

     .   .   .   .   .

I am sitting in my dingy little office, where a stingy
   Ray of sunlight struggles feebly down between the houses tall,
And the foetid air and gritty of the dusty, dirty city,
   Through the open window floating, spreads its foulness over all.

And in place of lowing cattle, I can hear the fiendish rattle
   Of the tramways and the buses making hurry down the street;
And the language uninviting of the gutter children fighting
   Comes fitfully and faintly through the ceaseless tramp of feet.

And the hurrying people daunt me, and their pallid faces haunt me
   As they shoulder one another in their rush and nervous haste,
With their eager eyes and greedy, and their stunted forms and
      weedy,
   For townsfolk have no time to grow, they have no time to waste.

And I somehow rather fancy that I'd like to change with Clancy,
   Like to take a turn at droving where the seasons come and go,
While he faced the round eternal of the cash-book and the journal—
   But I doubt he'd suit the office, Clancy, of The Overflow.

CLANCY OF THE OVERFLOW
Oil on canvas board 18in. × 14in. 1974

Geebung Polo Club

It was somewhere up the country, in a land of rock and scrub,
That they formed an institution called the Geebung Polo Club.
They were long and wiry natives from the rugged mountain side,
And the horse was never saddled that the Geebungs couldn't ride;
But their style of playing polo was irregular and rash—
They had mighty little science, but a mighty lot of dash:
And they played on mountain ponies that were muscular and
    strong,
Though their coats were quite unpolished, and their manes and tails
    were long.
And they used to train those ponies wheeling cattle in the scrub;
They were demons, were the members of the Geebung Polo Club.

It was somewhere down the country, in a city's smoke and steam,
That a polo club existed, called "The Cuff and Collar Team".
As a social institution 'twas a marvellous success,
For the members were distinguished by exclusiveness and dress.
They had natty little ponies that were nice, and smooth, and sleek,
For their cultivated owners only rode 'em once a week.
So they started up the country in pursuit of sport and fame,
For they meant to show the Geebungs how they ought to play
    the game;
And they took their valets with them—just to give their boots a rub
Ere they started operations on the Geebung Polo Club.

Now my readers can imagine how the contest ebbed and flowed,
When the Geebung boys got going it was time to clear the road;
And the game was so terrific that ere half the time was gone
A spectator's leg was broken—just from merely looking on.
For they waddied one another till the plain was strewn with dead,
While the score was kept so even that they neither got ahead.
And the Cuff and Collar Captain, when he tumbled off to die
Was the last surviving player—so the game was called a tie.
Then the Captain of the Geebungs raised him slowly from the
    ground,
Though his wounds were mostly mortal, yet he fiercely gazed
    around;
There was no one to oppose him—all the rest were in a trance,
So he scrambled on his pony for his last expiring chance,
For he meant to make an effort to get victory to his side;
So he struck at goal—and missed it—then he tumbled off and died.

      ·   ·   ·   ·   ·   ·

By the old Campaspe River, where the breezes shake the grass,
There's a row of little gravestones that the stockmen never pass,
For they bear a rude inscription saying, "Stranger, drop a tear,
For the Cuff and Collar players and the Geebung boys lie here."
And on misty moonlit evenings, while the dingoes howl around,
You can see their shadows flitting down that phantom polo ground;
You can hear the loud collisions as the flying players meet,
And the rattle of the mallets, and the rush of ponies' feet,
Till the terrified spectator rides like blazes to the pub—
He's been haunted by the spectres of the Geebung Polo Club.

GEEBUNG POLO CLUB
Oil on canvas board 18in. × 14in. 1974

Lost

"HE ought to be home," said the old man. "without there's something amiss.
He only went to the Two-mile—he ought to be back by this.
He *would* ride the Reckless filly, he *would* have his wilful way;
And here, he's not back at sundown—and what will his mother say?

"He was always his mother's idol, since ever his father died;
And there isn't a horse on the station that he isn't game to ride.
But that Reckless mare is vicious, and if once she gets away
He hasn't got strength to hold her—and what will his mother say?"

The old man walked to the sliprail, and peered up the darkening track,
And looked and longed for the rider that would never more come back;
And the mother came and clutched him, with sudden, spasmodic fright:
"What has become of my Willie?—why isn't he home tonight?"

Away in the gloomy ranges, at the foot of an ironbark,
The bonnie, winsome laddie was lying stiff and stark;
For the Reckless mare had smashed him against a leaning limb,
And his comely face was battered, and his merry eyes were dim.

And the thoroughbred chestnut filly, the saddle beneath her flanks,
Was away like fire through the ranges to join the wild mob's ranks;
And a broken-hearted woman and an old man worn and white
Were searching all day in the ranges till the sundown brought the night.

And the mother kept feebly calling, with a hope that would not die,
"Willie! where are you, Willie?" But how can the dead reply?
And hope died out with the daylight, and the darkness brought despair.
God pity the stricken mother, and answer the widow's prayer!

Though far and wide they sought him, they found not where he fell;
For the ranges held him precious, and guarded their treasure well.
The wattle blooms above him, and the blue bells blow close by,
And the brown bees buzz the secret, and the wild birds sing reply.

LOST
Oil on canvas board 18in. × 14in. 1974

But the mother pined and faded, and cried, and took no rest,
And rode each day to the ranges on her hopeless, weary quest,
Seeking her loved one ever, she faded and pined away,
But with strength of her great affection she still sought every day.

"I know that sooner or later I shall find my boy," she said.
But she came not home one evening, and they found her lying dead,
And stamped on the poor pale features, as the spirit homeward
        passed,
Was an angel smile of gladness—she had found her boy at last.

The Man From Snowy River

THERE was movement at the station, for the word had passed around
    That the colt from old Regret had got away,
And had joined the wild bush horses—he was worth a thousand pound,
    So all the cracks had gathered to the fray.
All the tried and noted riders from the stations near and far
    Had mustered at the homestead overnight,
For the bushmen love hard riding where the wild bush horses are,
    And the stock-horse snuffs the battle with delight.

There was Harrison, who made his pile when Pardon won the cup,
    The old man with his hair as white as snow;
But few could ride beside him when his blood was fairly up—
    He would go wherever horse and man could go.
And Clancy of the Overflow came down to lend a hand,
    No better horseman ever held the reins;
For never horse could throw him while the saddle-girths would stand—
    He learnt to ride while droving on the plains.

And one was there, a stripling on a small and weedy beast;
    He was something like a racehorse undersized,
With a touch of Timor pony—three parts thoroughbred at least—
    And such as are by mountain horsemen prized.
He was hard and tough and wiry—just the sort that won't say die—
    There was courage in his quick impatient tread;
And he bore the badge of gameness in his bright and fiery eye,
    And the proud and lofty carriage of his head.

But still so slight and weedy, one would doubt his power to stay,
    And the old man said, "That horse will never do
For a long and tiring gallop—lad, you'd better stop away,
    Those hills are far too rough for such as you."
So he waited, sad and wistful—only Clancy stood his friend—
    "I think we ought to let him come," he said:
"I warrant he'll be with us when he's wanted at the end,
    For both his horse and he are mountain bred.

"He hails from Snowy River, up by Kosciusko's side,
    Where the hills are twice as steep and twice as rough;
Where a horse's hoofs strike firelight from the flint stones every stride,
    The man that holds his own is good enough.
And the Snowy River riders on the mountains make their home,
    Where the river runs those giant hills between;
I have seen full many horsemen since I first commenced to roam,
But nowhere yet such horsemen have I seen."

So he went; they found the horses by the big mimosa clump,
　　They raced away towards the mountain's brow,
And the old man gave his orders, "Boys, go at them from the jump,
　　No use to try for fancy riding now.
And, Clancy, you must wheel them, try and wheel them to the right.
　　Ride boldly, lad, and never fear the spills,
For never yet was rider that could keep the mob in sight,
　　If once they gain the shelter of those hills."

So Clancy rode to wheel them—he was racing on the wing
　　Where the best and boldest riders take their place,
And he raced his stock-horse past them, and he made the ranges ring
　　With the stockwhip, as he met them face to face.
Then they halted for a moment, while he swung the dreaded lash,
　　But they saw their well-loved mountain full in view,
And they charged beneath the stockwhip with a sharp and sudden
　　　　dash,
　　And off into the mountain scrub they flew.

Then fast the horsemen followed, where the gorges deep and black
　　Resounded to the thunder of their tread,
And the stockwhips woke the echoes, and they fiercely answered
　　　　back
　　From cliffs and crags that beetled overhead.
And upward, ever upward, the wild horses held their way,
　　Where mountain ash and kurrajong grew wide;
And the old man muttered fiercely, "We may bid the mob good day,
　　No man can hold them down the other side."

When they reached the mountain's summit, even Clancy took a
　　　　pull—
　　It well might make the boldest hold their breath;
The wild hop scrub grew thickly, and the hidden ground was full
　　Of wombat holes, and any slip was death.

But the man from Snowy River let the pony have his head,
　　And he swung his stockwhip round and gave a cheer,
And he raced him down the mountain like a torrent down its bed,
　　While the others stood and watched in very fear.

He sent the flint-stones flying, but the pony kept his feet,
　　He cleared the fallen timber in his stride,
And the man from Snowy River never shifted in his seat—
　　It was grand to see that mountain horseman ride.
Through the stringy barks and saplings, on the rough and broken
　　　　ground,
　　Down the hillside at a racing pace he went;
And he never drew the bridle till he landed safe and sound
　　At the bottom of that terrible descent.

THE MAN FROM SNOWY RIVER
Oil on canvas board 18in. × 14in. 1974

He was right among the horses as they climbed the farther hill,
    And the watchers on the mountain, standing mute,
Saw him ply the stockwhip fiercely; he was right among them still,
    As he raced across the clearing in pursuit.
Then they lost him for a moment, where two mountain gullies met
    In the ranges—but a final glimpse reveals
On a dim and distant hillside the wild horses racing yet,
    With the man from Snowy River at their heels.

And he ran them single-handed till their sides were white with foam;
    He followed like a bloodhound on their track,
Till they halted, cowed and beaten; then he turned their heads for
      home,
    And alone and unassisted brought them back.
But his hardy mountain pony he could scarcely raise a trot,
    He was blood from hip to shoulder from the spur;
But his pluck was still undaunted, and his courage fiery hot,
    For never yet was mountain horse a cur.

And down by Kosciusko, where the pine-clad ridges raise
    Their torn and rugged battlements on high,
Where the air is clear as crystal, and the white stars fairly blaze
    At midnight in the cold and frosty sky,
And where around the Overflow the reed-beds sweep and sway
    To the breezes, and the rolling plains are wide,
The Man from Snowy River is a household word today,
    And the stockmen tell the story of his ride.

THE MAN FROM SNOWY RIVER
Oil on canvas board 18in. × 14in. 1974

The Swagman's Rest

WE buried old Bob where the bloodwoods wave
    At the foot of the Eaglehawk;
We fashioned a cross on the old man's grave
    For fear that his ghost might walk;
We carved his name on a bloodwood tree
    With the date of his sad decease
And in place of "Died from effects of spree"
    We wrote "May he rest in peace".

For Bob was known on the Overland,
    A regular old bush wag,
Tramping along in the dust and sand,
    Humping his well-worn swag.
He would camp for days in the river-bed,
    And loiter and "fish for whales".
"I'm into the swagman's yard," he said.
    "And I never shall find the rails."

But he found the rails on that summer night
    For a better place—or worse,
As we watched by turns in the flickering light
    With an old black gin for nurse.
The breeze came in with the scent of pine,
    The river sounded clear,
When a change came on, and we saw the sign
    That told us the end was near.

He spoke in a cultured voice and low—
    "I fancy they've 'sent the route';
I once was an army man, you know.
    Though now I'm a drunken brute;
But bury me out where the bloodwoods wave,
    And, if ever you're fairly stuck,
Just take and shovel me out of the grave
    And, maybe, I'll bring you luck.

THE SWAGMAN'S REST
Oil on hardboard 18in. × 14in. 1974

"For I've always heard—" here his voice grew weak,
  His strength was wellnigh sped,
He gasped and struggled and tried to speak,
  Then fell in a moment—dead.
Thus ended a wasted life and hard,
  Of energies misapplied—
Old Bob was out of the "swagman's yard"
  And over the Great Divide.

.   .   .   .   .

The drought came down on the field and flock,
  And never a raindrop fell,
Though the tortured moans of the starving stock
  Might soften a fiend from hell.
And we thought of the hint that the swagman gave
  When he went to the Great Unseen—
We shovelled the skeleton out of the grave
  To see what his hint might mean.

We dug where the cross and the grave posts were,
  We shovelled away the mould,
When sudden a vein of quartz lay bare
  All gleaming with yellow gold.
'Twas a reef with never a fault nor baulk
  That ran from the range's crest,
And the richest mine on the Eaglehawk
  Is known as "The Swagman's Rest".

The Road to Hogan's Gap

Now look, you see, it's this way like—
    You cross the broken bridge
And run the crick down, till you strike
    The second right-hand ridge.

The track is hard to see in parts,
    But still it's pretty clear;
There's been two Injun hawkers' carts
    Along that road this year.

Well, run that right-hand ridge along—
    It ain't, to say, too steep—
There's two fresh tracks might put you wrong
    Where blokes went out with sheep.

But keep the crick upon your right,
    And follow pretty straight
Along the spur, until you sight
    A wire and sapling gate.

Well, that's where Hogan's old grey mare
    Fell off and broke her back;
You'll see her carcass layin' there,
    Jist down below the track.

And then you drop two mile, or three,
    It's pretty steep and blind;
You want to go and fall a tree
    And tie it on behind.

And then you pass a broken cart
    Below a granite bluff;
And that is where you strike the part
    They reckon pretty rough.

But by the time you've got that far
    It's either cure or kill,
So turn your horses round the spur
    And face 'em up the hill.

For look, if you should miss the slope
    And get below the track,
You haven't got the slightest hope
    Of ever gettin' back.

An' half way up you'll see the hide
    Of Hogan's brindled bull;
Well, mind and keep the right-hand side.
    The left's too steep a pull.

And both the banks is full of cracks;
  An' just about at dark
You'll see the last year's bullock tracks
  Where Hogan drew the bark.

The marks is old and pretty faint—
  O'ergrown with scrub and such;
Of course the track to Hogan's ain't
  A road that's travelled much.

But turn and run the tracks along
  For half a mile or more,
And then, of course, you can't go wrong—
  You're right at Hogan's door.

When first you come to Hogan's gate
  He mightn't show perhaps;
He's pretty sure to plant, and wait
  To see it ain't the traps.

I wouldn't call it good enough
  To let your horses out;
There's some that's pretty extra rough
  Is livin' round about.

It's likely, if your horses did
  Get feedin' near the track
It's going to cost at least a quid
  Or more to get them back.

So, if you find they're off the place,
  It's up to you to go
And flash a quid in Hogan's face—
  He'll know the blokes that know.

But listen—if you're feelin' dry,
  Just see there's no one near,
And go and wink the other eye
  And ask for ginger beer.

The blokes come in from near and far
  To sample Hogan's pop;
They reckon once they breast the bar
  They stay there till they drop.

On Sundays you can see them spread
  Like flies around the tap.
It's like that song "The Livin' Dead"
  Up there at Hogan's Gap.

THE ROAD TO HOGAN'S GAP
Oil on hardboard 18in. × 14in. 1974

They like to make it pretty strong
  Whenever there's a chance;
So when a stranger comes along
  They always hold a dance.

There's recitations, songs, and fights—
  A willin' lot you'll meet.
There's one long bloke up there recites;
  I tell you he's a treat.

They're lively blokes all right up there,
  It's never dull a day.
I'd go meself if I could spare
  The time to get away.

    .   .   .   .   .

The stranger turned his horses quick.
  He didn't cross the bridge;
He didn't go along the crick
  To strike the second ridge;

He didn't make the trip, because
  He wasn't feeling fit.
His business up at Hogan's was
  To serve him with a writ.

He reckoned, if he faced the pull
  And climbed the rocky stair,
The next to come might find his hide
A landmark on the mountain side,
Along with Hogan's brindled bull
  And Hogan's old grey mare!

THE ROAD TO HOGAN'S GAP
Oil on canvas board 16in. × 13½in. 1974

Song of the Wheat

WE have sung the song of the droving days,
  Of the march of the travelling sheep—
How by silent stages and lonely ways
  Thin, white battalions creep.
But the man who now by the land would thrive
  Must his spurs to a ploughshare beat;
And the bush bard, changing his tune, may strive
  To sing the song of the Wheat!

It's west by south of the Great Divide
  The grim grey plains run out,
Where the old flock-masters lived and died
  In a ceaseless fight with drought.
Weary with waiting and hope deferred
  They were ready to own defeat,
Till at last they heard the master-word—
  And the master-word was Wheat.

Yarran and Myall and Box and Pine—
  'Twas axe and fire for all;
They scarce could tarry to blaze the line
  Or wait for the trees to fall
Ere the team was yoked, and the gates flung wide,
  And the dust of the horses' feet
Rose up like a pillar of smoke to guide
  The wonderful march of Wheat.

Furrow by furrow, and fold by fold,
  The soil is turned on the plain;
Better than silver and better than gold
  Is the surface-mine of the grain.
Better than cattle and better than sheep
  In the fight with drought and heat;
For a streak of stubbornness, wide and deep,
  Lies hid in a grain of Wheat.

When the stock is swept by the hand of fate,
  Deep down on his bed of clay
The brave brown Wheat will die and wait
  For the resurrection day—
Lie hid while the whole world thinks him dead;
  But the Spring-rain, soft and sweet,
Will over the steaming paddocks spread
  The first green flush of the Wheat.

SONG OF THE WHEAT
Oil on hardboard 18in. × 14in. 1974

Green and amber and gold it grows
  When the sun sinks late in the West;
And the breeze sweeps over the rippling rows
  Where the quail and the skylark nest.
Mountain or river or shining star,
  There's never a sight can beat—
Away to the sky-line stretching far—
  A sea of the ripening Wheat.

When the burning harvest sun sinks low,
  And shadows stretch on the plain,
The roaring strippers come and go
  Like ships on a sea of grain.
Till the lurching, groaning waggons bear
  Their tale of the load complete.
Of the world's great work he has done his share
  Who has garnered a crop of wheat.

Princes, Potentates, Kings and Czars,
  They travel in regal state,
But old King Wheat has a thousand cars
  For his trip to the water-gate;
And his thousand steamships breast the tide
  And plough through the wind and sleet
To the lands where the teeming millions bide
  That say: "Thank God for Wheat!"

Mulga Bill's Bicycle

'Twas Mulga Bill, from Eaglehawk, that caught the cycling craze;
He turned away the good old horse that served him many days;
He dressed himself in cycling clothes, resplendent to be seen;
He hurried off to town and bought a shining new machine;
And as he wheeled it through the door, with air of lordly pride,
The grinning shop assistant said, "Excuse me, can you ride?"

"See here, young man," said Mulga Bill, "from Walgett to the sea,
From Conroy's Gap to Castlereagh, there's none can ride like me.
I'm good all round at everything, as everybody knows,
Although I'm not the one to talk—I hate a man that blows.

"But riding is my special gift, my chiefest, sole delight;
Just ask a wild duck can it swim, a wild cat can it fight.
There's nothing clothed in hair or hide, or built of flesh or steel,
There's nothing walks or jumps, or runs, on axle, hoof, or wheel,
But what I'll sit, while hide will hold and girths and straps are tight;
I'll ride this here two-wheeled concern right straight away at sight."

'Twas Mulga Bill, from Eaglehawk, that sought his own abode,
That perched above the Dead Man's Creek, beside the mountain
     road.
He turned the cycle down the hill and mounted for the fray,
But ere he'd gone a dozen yards it bolted clean away.
It left the track, and through the trees, just like a silver streak,
It whistled down the awful slope towards the Dead Man's Creek.

It shaved a stump by half an inch, it dodged a big white-box:
The very wallaroos in fright went scrambling up the rocks,
The wombats hiding in their caves dug deeper underground,
But Mulga Bill, as white as chalk, sat tight to every bound.
It struck a stone and gave a spring that cleared a fallen tree,
It raced beside a precipice as close as close could be;
And then, as Mulga Bill let out one last despairing shriek,
It made a leap of twenty feet into the Dead Man's Creek.

'Twas Mulga Bill, from Eaglehawk, that slowly swam ashore:
He said, "I've had some narrer shaves and lively rides before;
I've rode a wild bull round a yard to win a five-pound bet,
But this was sure the derndest ride that I've encountered yet.
I'll give that two-wheeled outlaw best; it's shaken all my nerve
To feel it whistle through the air and plunge and buck, and swerve,
It's safe at rest in Dead Man's Creek—we'll leave it lying still;
A horse's back is good enough henceforth for Mulga Bill."

MULGA BILL'S BICYCLE
Oil on canvas board 18in. × 14in. 1974

Waltzing Matilda

(Carrying a Swag)

OH! there once was a swagman camped in a Billabong,
    Under the shade of a Coolabah tree;
And he sang as he looked at his old billy boiling,
    "Who'll come a-waltzing Matilda with me?"

    Who'll come a-waltzing Matilda, my darling,
        Who'll come a-waltzing Matilda with me?
    Waltzing Matilda and leading a water-bag—
        Who'll come a-waltzing Matilda with me?

Down came a jumbuck to drink at the water-hole,
    Up jumped the swagman and grabbed him in glee;
And he sang as he stowed him away in his tucker-bag,
    "You'll come a-waltzing Matilda with me."

Down came the Squatter a-riding his thoroughbred;
    Down came Policemen—one, two and three.
      "Whose is the jumbuck you've got in the tucker-bag?
    You'll come a-waltzing Matilda with me."

But the swagman, he up and he jumped in the water-hole,
    Drowning himself by the Coolabah tree;
And his ghost may be heard as it sings in the Billabong
    "Who'll come a-waltzing Matilda with me?"

WALTZING MATILDA
Oil on hardboard 18in. × 14in. 1974

Saltbush Bill

Now this is the law of the Overland that all in the West obey—
A man must cover with travelling sheep a six-mile stage a day;
But this is the law which the drovers make, right easily understood,
They travel their stage where the grass is bad, but they camp
    where the grass is good;
They camp, and they ravage the squatter's grass till never a
    blade remains.
Then they drift away as the white clouds drift on the edge of the
    saltbush plains:
From camp to camp and from run to run they battle it hand to
    hand
For a blade of grass and the right to pass on the track of the
    Overland.
For this is the law of the Great Stock Routes, 'tis written in
    white and black—
The man that goes with a travelling mob must keep to a half-mile
    track;
And the drovers keep to a half-mile track on the runs where the
    grass is dead,
But they spread their sheep on a well-grassed run till they go
    with a two-mile spread.
So the squatters hurry the drovers on from dawn till the fall of
    night,
And the squatters' dogs and the drovers' dogs get mixed in a
    deadly fight.
Yet the squatters' men, though they haunt the mob, are willing
    the peace to keep,
For the drovers learn how to use their hands when they go with
    the travelling sheep;
But this is the tale of a Jackeroo that came from a foreign strand,
And the fight that he fought with Saltbush Bill, the King of
    the Overland.

Now Saltbush Bill was a drover tough as ever the country knew,
He had fought his way on the Great Stock Routes from the sea
    to the big Barcoo;
He could tell when he came to a friendly run that gave him a
    chance to spread,
And he knew where the hungry owners were that hurried his
    sheep ahead;
He was drifting down in the Eighty drought with a mob that
    could scarcely creep
(When the kangaroos by the thousand starve, it is rough on the
    travelling sheep),

SALTBUSH BILL
Oil on canvas board 18in. × 14in. 1974

And he camped one night at the crossing-place on the edge of
the Wilga run;
"We must manage a feed for them here," he said, "or half of the
mob are done!"
So he spread them out when they left the camp wherever they
liked to go,
Till he grew aware of a Jackeroo with a station-hand in tow.
They set to work on the straggling sheep, and with many a stock-
whip crack
They forced them in where the grass was dead in the space of
the half-mile track;
And William prayed that the hand of Fate might suddenly strike
him blue
But he'd get some grass for his starving sheep in the teeth of that
Jackeroo.
So he turned and he cursed the Jackeroo; he cursed him, alive
or dead,
From the soles of his great unwieldly feet to the crown of his
ugly head,
With an extra curse on the moke he rode and the cur at his heels
that ran,
Till the Jackaroo from his horse got down and went for the drover-
man;
With the station-hand for his picker-up, though the sheep ran
loose the while,
They battled it out on the well-grassed plain in the regular prize-
ring style.

Now, the new chum fought for his honour's sake and the pride
of the English race,
But the drover fought for his daily bread with a smile on his
bearded face;
So he shifted ground, and he sparred for wind, and he made it
a lengthy mill,
And from time to time as his scouts came in they whispered to
Saltbush Bill—
"We have spread the sheep with a two-mile spread, and the grass
it is something grand;
You must stick to him, Bill, for another round for the pride of
the Overland."

The new chum made it a rushing fight, though never a blow
    got home,
Till the sun rode high in the cloudless sky and glared on the
    brick-red loam,
Till the sheep drew in to the shelter-trees and settled them down
    to rest;
Then the drover said he would fight no more, and gave his
    opponent best.

So the new chum rode to the homestead straight, and told them a
    story grand
Of the desperate fight that he fought that day with the King
    of the Overland;
And the tale went home to the Public Schools of the pluck of the
    English swell—
How the drover fought for his very life, but blood in the end
    must tell.
But the travelling sheep and the Wilga sheep were boxed on the
    Old Man Plain;
'Twas a full week's work ere they drafted out and hunted them
    off again;
A week's good grass in their wretched hides, with a curse and a
    stockwhip crack
They hunted them off on the road once more to starve on the
    half-mile track.
And Saltbush Bill, on the Overland, will many a time recite
How the best day's work that he ever did was the day that he
    lost the fight.

In Defence of the Bush

So you're back from up the country, Mister Lawson, where you
    went,
And you're cursing all the business in a bitter discontent;
Well, we grieve to disappoint you, and it makes us sad to hear
That it wasn't cool and shady—and there wasn't whips of beer,
And the looney bullock snorted when you first came into view—
Well, you know it's not so often that he sees a swell like you;
And the roads were hot and dusty, and the plains were burnt
    and brown,
And no doubt you're better suited drinking lemon-squash in town.
Yet, perchance, if you should journey down the very track you
    went
In a month or two at furthest, you would wonder what it meant;
Where the sunbaked earth was gasping like a creature in its pain
You would find the grasses waving like a field of summer grain,
And the miles of thirsty gutters, blocked with sand and choked
    with mud,
You would find them mighty rivers with a turbid, sweeping flood.
For the rain and drought and sunshine make no changes in the
    street,
In the sullen line of buildings and the ceaseless tramp of feet;
But the bush has moods and changes, as the seasons rise and fall,
And the men who know the bush-land—they are loyal through it all.

· · · · · · ·

But you found the bush was dismal and a land of no delight—
Did you chance to hear a chorus in the shearers' huts at night?
Did they "rise up William Riley" by the camp-fire's cheery blaze?
Did they rise him as we rose him in the good old droving days?
And the women of the homesteads and the men you chanced to
    meet—
Were their faces sour and saddened like the "faces in the street"?
And the "shy selector children"—were they better now or worse
Than the little city urchins who would greet you with a curse?
Is not such a life much better than the squalid street and square
Where the fallen women flaunt it in the fierce electric glare,
Where the sempstress plies her needle till her eyes are sore and red
In a filthy, dirty attic toiling on for daily bread?

IN DEFENCE OF THE BUSH
Oil on canvas board 18in. × 14in. 1974

Did you hear no sweeter voices in the music of the bush
Than the roar of trams and buses, and the war-whoop of "the push"?
Did the magpies rouse your slumbers with their carol sweet and
    strange?
Did you hear the silver chiming of the bell-birds on the range?
But, perchance, the wild birds' music by your senses was despised,
For you say you'll stay in townships till the bush is civilized.
Would you make it a tea-garden, and on Sundays have a band
Where the "blokes" might take their "donahs", with a "public"
    close at hand?
You had better stick to Sydney and make merry with the "push",
For the bush will never suit you, and you'll never suit the bush.

When Dacey Rode the Mule

'TWAS to a small, up-country town,
  When we were boys at school,
There came a circus with a clown,
  Likewise a bucking mule.
The clown announced a scheme they had
  Spectators for to bring—
They'd give a crown to any lad
  Who'd ride him round the ring.

And, gentle reader, do not scoff
  Nor think a man a fool—
To buck a porous-plaster off
  Was pastime to that mule.

The boys got on he bucked like sin;
  He threw them in the dirt.
What time the clown would raise a grin
  By asking, "Are you hurt?"
But Johnny Dacey came one night,
  The crack of all the school;
Said he, "I'll win the crown all right;
  Bring in your bucking mule."

The elephant went off his trunk,
  The monkey played the fool,
And all the band got blazing drunk
  When Dacey rode the mule.

But soon there rose a galling shout
  Of laughter, for the clown
From somewhere in his pants drew out
  A little paper crown.
He placed the crown on Dacey's head
  While Dacey looked a fool;
"Now, there's your crown, my lad," he said,
  "For riding of the mule!"

The band struck up with "Killaloe",
  And "Rule Britannia, Rule",
And "Young Man from the Country", too,
  When Dacey rode the mule.
Then Dacey, in a furious rage,
  For vengeance on the show
Ascended to the monkeys' cage
  And let the monkeys go;
The blue-tailed ape and the chimpanzee
  He turned abroad to roam;
Good faith! It was a sight to see
  The people step for home.

For big baboons with canine snout
　　Are spiteful, as a rule—
The people didn't sit it out,
　　When Dacey rode the mule.

And from the beasts he let escape,
　　The bushmen all declare,
Were·born some creatures partly ape
　　And partly native-bear.
They're rather few and far between,
　　The race is nearly spent;
But some of them may still be seen
　　In Sydney Parliament.

And when those legislators fight,
　　And drink, and act the fool,
Just blame it on that torrid night
　　When Dacey rode the mule.

WHEN DACEY RODE THE MULE
Oil on canvas board 18in. × 14in. 1974

Shearing at Castlereagh

THE bell is set a-ringing, and the engine gives a toot,
There's five-and-thirty shearers here a-shearing for the loot,
So stir yourselves, you penners-up, and shove the sheep along—
The musterers are fetching them a hundred thousand strong—
And make your collie dogs speak up; what would the buyers say
In London if the wool was late this year from Castlereagh?

The man that "rung" the Tubbo shed is not the ringer here,
That stripling from the Cooma-side can teach him how to shear.
They trim away the ragged locks, and rip the cutter goes,
And leaves a track of snowy fleece from brisket to the nose;
It's lovely how they peel it off with never stop nor stay,
They're racing for the ringer's place this year at Castlereagh.

The man that keeps the cutters sharp is growling in his cage,
He's always in a hurry; and he's always in a rage—
"You clumsy-fisted mutton-heads, you'd turn a fellow sick,
You pass yourselves as shearers, you were born to swing a pick.
Another broken cutter here, that's two you've broke today,
It's lovely how they peel it off with never stop nor stay,

The youngsters picking up the fleece enjoy the merry din,
They throw the classer up the fleece, he throws it to the bin;
The pressers standing by the rack are waiting for the wool,
There's room for just a couple more, the press is nearly full;
Now jump upon the lever, lads, and heave and heave away,
Another bale of golden fleece is branded "Castlereagh".

SHEARING AT CASTLEREAGH
Oil on canvas board 18in. × 14in. 1974

The First Surveyor

"THE opening of the railway line!—the Governor and all!
With flags and banners down the street, a banquet and a ball.
Hark to 'em at the station now! They're raising cheer on cheer!
'The man who brought the railway through—our friend the
      engineer.'

"They cheer *his* pluck and enterprise and engineering skill!
'Twas my old husband found the pass behind that big red hill.
Before the engineer was born we'd settled with our stock
Behind that great big mountain chain, a line of range and rock—
A line that kept us starving there in weary weeks of drought,
With ne'er a track across the range to let the cattle out.

" 'Twas then, with horses starved and weak and scarcely fit to crawl,
My husband went to find a way across the rocky wall.
He vanished in the wilderness—God knows where he was gone—
He hunted till his food gave out, but still he battled on.
His horses strayed ('twas well they did), they made towards the
      grass,
And down behind that big red hill they found an easy pass.

"He followed up and blazed the trees, to show the safest track,
Then drew his belt another hole and turned and started back.
His horses died—just one pulled through with nothing much to
      spare;
God bless the beast that brought him home, the old white Arab
      mare!
We drove the cattle through the hills, along the new-found way,
And this was our first camping-ground—just where I live today.

"Then others came across the range and built the township here,
And then there came the railway line and this young engineer;
He drove about with tents and traps, a cook to cook his meals,
A bath to wash himself at night, a chain-man at his heels.
And that was all the pluck and skill for which he's cheered and
      praised,
For after all he took the track, the same my husband blazed!

"My poor old husband, dead and gone with never feast nor cheer;
He's buried by the railway line!—I wonder can he hear
When by the very track he marked, and close to where he's laid,
The cattle trains go roaring down the one-in-thirty grade.
I wonder does he hear them pass, and can he see the sight
When, whistling shrill, the fast express goes flaming by at night.

THE FIRST SURVEYOR
Oil on canvas board 18in. × 14in. 1974

"I think 'twould comfort him to know there's someone left to care;
I'll take some things this very night and hold a banquet there—
The hard old fare we've often shared together, him and me,
Some damper and a bite of beef, a pannikin of tea:
We'll do without the bands and flags, the speeches and the fuss,
We know who *ought* to get the cheers—and that's enough for us.

"What's that? They wish that I'd come down—the oldest settler here!
Present me to the Governor and that young engineer!
Well, just you tell his Excellence, and put the thing polite,
I'm sorry, but I can't come down—I'm dining out tonight!"

How Gilbert Died

THERE'S never a stone at the sleeper's head,
  There's never a fence beside,
And the wandering stock on the grave may tread
  Unnoticed and undenied;
But the smallest child on the Watershed
  Can tell you how Gilbert died.

For he rode at dusk with his comrade Dunn
  To the hut at the Stockman's Ford;
In the waning light of the sinking sun
  They peered with a fierce accord.
They were outlaws both—and on each man's head
  Was a thousand pounds reward.

They had taken toll of the country round,
  And the troopers came behind
With a black who tracked like a human hound
  In the scrub and the ranges blind:
He could run the trail where a white man's eye
  No sign of track could find.

He had hunted them out of the One Tree Hill
  And over the Old Man Plain,
But they wheeled their tracks with a wild beast's skill,
  And they made for the range again;
Then away to the hut where their grandsire dwelt
  They rode with a loosened rein.

And their grandsire gave them a greeting bold:
  "Come in and rest in peace,
No safer place does the country hold—
  With the night pursuit must cease,
And we'll drink success to the roving boys,
  And to hell with the black police."

But they went to death when they entered there
  In the hut at the Stockman's Ford,
For their grandsire's words were as false as fair—
  They were doomed to the hangman's cord.
He had sold them both to the black police
  For the sake of the big reward.

In the depth of night there are forms that glide
  As stealthily as serpents creep,
And around the hut where the outlaws hide
  They plant in the shadows deep,
And they wait till the first faint flush of dawn
  Shall waken their prey from sleep.

But Gilbert wakes while the night is dark—
　　A restless sleeper aye.
He has heard the sound of a sheep-dog's bark,
　　And his horse's warning neigh,
And he says to his mate, "There are hawks abroad,
　　And it's time that we went away."

Their rifles stood at the stretcher head,
　　Their bridles lay to hand;
They wakened the old man out of his bed,
　　When they heard the sharp command:
"In the name of the Queen lay down your arms,
　　Now, Dunn and Gilbert, stand!"

Then Gilbert reached for his rifle true
　　That close at hand he kept;
He pointed straight at the voice, and drew,
　　But never a flash outleapt,
For the water ran from the rifle breech—
　　It was drenched while the outlaws slept.

Then he dropped the piece with a bitter oath,
　　And he turned to his comrade Dunn:
"We are sold," he said, "we are dead men both!—
　　Still, there may be a chance for one;
I'll stop and I'll fight with the pistol here,
　　You take to your heels and run."

So Dunn crept out on his hands and knees
　　In the dim, half-dawning light,
And he made his way to a patch of trees,
　　And was lost in the black of night;
And the trackers hunted his tracks all day,
　　But they never could trace his flight.

But Gilbert walked from the open door
　　In a confident style and rash;
He heard at his side the rifles roar,
　　And he heard the bullets crash.
But he laughed as he lifted his pistol-hand,
　　And he fired at the rifle flash.

Then out of the shadows the troopers aimed
　　At his voice and the pistol sound.
With rifle flashes the darkness flamed—
　　He staggered and spun around,
And they riddled his body with rifle balls
　　As it lay on the blood-soaked ground.

HOW GILBERT DIED
Oil on canvas board 18in. × 14in. 1974

There's never a stone at the sleeper's head,
   There's never a fence beside,
And the wandering stock on the grave may tread
   Unnoticed and undenied;
But the smallest child on the Watershed
   Can tell you how Gilbert died.

The Man From Ironbark

It was the man from Ironbark who struck the Sydney town,
He wandered over street and park, he wandered up and down.
He loitered here, he loitered there, till he was like to drop,
Until at last in sheer despair he sought a barber's shop.
" 'Ere! shave my beard and whiskers off, I'll be a man of mark,
I'll go and do the Sydney toff up home in Ironbark."

The barber man was small and flash, as barbers mostly are,
He wore a strike-your-fancy sash, he smoked a huge cigar:
He was a humorist of note and keen at repartee,
He laid the odds and kept a "tote", whatever that may be.
And when he saw our friend arrive, he whispered "Here's a lark!
Just watch me catch him all alive this man from Ironbark."

There were some gilded youths that sat along the barber's wall,
Their eyes were dull, their heads were flat, they had no brains
        at all;
To them the barber passed the wink, his dexter eyelid shut,
"I'll make this bloomin' yokel think his bloomin' throat is cut."
And as he soaped and rubbed it in he made a rude remark:
"I s'pose the flats is pretty green up there in Ironbark."

A grunt was all reply he got; he shaved the bushman's chin,
Then made the water boiling hot and dipped the razor in.
He raised his hand, his brow grew black, he paused awhile to
        gloat,
Then slashed the red-hot razor-back across his victim's throat;
Upon the newly-shaven skin it made a livid mark—
No doubt it fairly took him in—the man from Ironbark.

He fetched a wild up-country yell might wake the dead to hear,
And though his throat, he knew full well, was cut from ear to ear,
He struggled gamely to his feet, and faced the murderous foe.
"You've done for me! you dog, I'm beat! one hit before I go!
I only wish I had a knife, you blessed murdering shark!
But you'll remember all your life the man from Ironbark."

He lifted up his hairy paw, with one tremendous clout
He landed on the barber's jaw, and knocked the barber out.
He set to work with tooth and nail, he made the place a wreck;
He grabbed the nearest gilded youth, and tried to break his neck.
And all the while his throat he held to save his vital spark,
And "Murder! Bloody Murder!" yelled the man from Ironbark.

A peeler man who heard the din came in to see the show;
He tried to run the bushman in, but he refused to go.
And when at last the barber spoke, and said " 'Twas all in fun—
'Twas just a little harmless joke, a trifle overdone."
"A joke!" he cried, "By George, that's fine; a lively sort of lark;
I'd like to catch that murdering swine some night in Ironbark."

And now while round the shearing-floor the listening shearers gape,
He tells the story o'er and o'er and brags of his escape.
"Them barber chaps what keeps a tote, by George, I've had enough,
One tried to cut my bloomin' throat, but thank the Lord it's tough."
And whether he's believed or no, there's one thing to remark,
That flowing beards are all the go way up in Ironbark.

THE MAN FROM IRONBARK
Oil on hardboard 18in. × 14in. 1974

A Bush Christening

ON the outer Barcoo where the churches are few,
  And men of religion are scanty,
On a road never cross'd 'cept by folk that are lost
  One Michael Magee had a shanty.

Now this Mike was the dad of a ten-year-old lad,
  Plump, healthy, and stoutly conditioned;
He was strong as the best, but poor Mike had no rest
  For the youngster had never been christened.

And his wife used to cry, "If the darlin' should die
  Saint Peter would not recognize him."
But by luck he survived till a preacher arrived,
  Who agreed straightaway to baptize him.

Now the artful young rogue, while they held their collogue,
  With his ear to the keyhole was listenin';
And he muttered in fright, while his features turned white,
  "What the devil and all is this christenin'?"

He was none of your dolts—he had seen them brand colts.
  And it seemed to his small understanding,
If the man in the frock made him one of the flock,
  It must mean something very like branding.

So away with a rush he set off for the bush,
  While the tears in his eyelids they glistened—
" 'Tis outrageous," says he, "to brand youngsters like me;
  I'll be dashed if I'll stop to be christened!"

Like a young native dog he ran into a log,
  And his father with language uncivil,
Never heeding the "praste", cried aloud in his haste
  "Come out and be christened, you divil!"

But he lay there as snug as a bug in a rug,
  And his parents in vain might reprove him,
Till his reverence spoke (he was fond of a joke)
  "I've a notion," says he, "that'll move him.

"Poke a stick up the log, give the spalpeen a prog;
  Poke him aisy—don't hurt him or maim him;
'Tis not long that he'll stand, I've the water at hand,
  As he rushes out this end I'll name him.

"Here he comes, and for shame! ye've forgotten the name—
  Is it Patsy or Michael or Dinnis?"
Here the youngster ran out, and the priest gave a shout—
  "Take your chance, anyhow, wid 'Maginnis!' "

A BUSH CHRISTENING
Oil on harboard 18in. × 24in. 1974

As the howling young cub ran away to the scrub
　　Where he knew that pursuit would be risky,
The priest, as he fled, flung a flask at his head
　　That was labelled "Maginnis's Whisky"!

Now Maginnis Magee has been made a J.P.,
　　And the one thing he hates more than sin is
To be asked by the folk, who have heard of the joke,
　　How he came to be christened Maginnis!

In the Droving Days

"ONLY a pound," said the auctioneer,
"Only a pound; and I'm standing here
Selling this animal, gain or loss—
Only a pound for the drover's horse?
One of the sort that was ne'er afraid,
One of the boys of the Old Brigade;
Thoroughly honest and game, I'll swear,
Only a little the worse for wear;
Plenty as bad to be seen in town,
Give me a bid and I'll knock him down;
Sold as he stands, and without recourse,
Give me a bid for the drover's horse."

Loitering there in an aimless way
Somehow I noticed the poor old grey,
Weary and battered and screwed, of course;
Yet when I noticed the old grey horse,
The rough bush saddle, and single rein
Of the bridle laid on his tangled mane,
Straightway the crowd and the auctioneer
Seemed on a sudden to disappear,
Melted away in a kind of haze—
For my heart went back to the droving days.

Back to the road, and I crossed again
Over the miles of the saltbush plain—
The shining plain that is said to be
The dried-up bed of an inland sea.
Where the air so dry and so clear and bright
Refracts the sun with a wondrous light,
And out in the dim horizon makes
The deep blue gleam of the phantom lakes.

At dawn of day we could feel the breeze
That stirred the boughs of the sleeping trees,
And brought a breath of the fragrance rare
That comes and goes in that scented air;
For the trees and grass and the shrubs contain
A dry sweet scent on the saltbush plain.
For those that love it and understand
The saltbush plain is a wonderland,
A wondrous country, where Nature's ways
Were revealed to me in the droving days.

We saw the fleet wild horses pass,
And kangaroos through the Mitchell grass;
The emu ran with her frightened brood
All unmolested and unpursued.
But there rose a shout and a wild hubbub
When the dingo raced for his native scrub,
And he paid right dear for his stolen meals
With the drovers' dogs at his wretched heels.
For we ran him down at a rattling pace,
While the pack-horse joined in the stirring chase.
And a wild halloo at the kill we'd raise—
We were light of heart in the droving days.

'Twas a drover's horse, and my hand again
Made a move to close on a fancied rein.
For I felt the swing and the easy stride
Of the grand old horse that I used to ride.
In drought or plenty, in good or ill,
The same old steed was my comrade still;
The old grey horse with his honest ways
Was a mate to me in the droving days.

When we kept our watch in the cold and damp,
If the cattle broke from the sleeping camp,
Over the flats and across the plain,
With my head bent down on his waving mane,
Through the boughs above and the stumps below,
On the darkest night I could let him go
At a racing speed; he would choose his course,
And my life was safe with the old grey horse.
But man and horse had a favourite job,
When an outlaw broke from a station mob;
With a right good will was the stockwhip plied,
As the old horse raced at the straggler's side,
And the greenhide whip such a weal would raise—
We could use the whip in the droving days.

      .   .   .   .   .

"Only a pound!" and was this the end—
Only a pound for the drover's friend.
The drover's friend that has seen his day,
And now was worthless and cast away
With a broken knee and a broken heart
To be flogged and starved in a hawker's cart.
Well, I made a bid for a sense of shame.
And the memories dear of the good old game.

IN THE DROVING DAYS
Oil on canvas board 18in. × 14in. 1974

"Thank you? Guinea! and cheap at that!
Against you there in the curly hat!
Only a guinea, and one more chance,
Down he goes if there's no advance,
Third, and last time, one! two! three!"
And the old grey horse was knocked down to me.
And now he's wandering, fat and sleek,
On the lucerne flats by the Homestead Creek;
I dare not ride him for fear he'd fall,
But he does a journey to beat them all,
For though he scarcely a trot can raise,
He can take me back to the droving days.

Song of the Artesian Water

Now the stock have started dying, for the Lord has sent a drought;
But we're sick of prayers and Providence—we're going to do without;
With the derricks up above us and the solid earth below,
We are waiting at the lever for the word to let her go.
   Sinking down, deeper down
   Oh, we'll sink it deeper down:
As the drill is plugging downward at a thousand feet of level,
If the Lord won't send us water, oh, we'll get it from the devil;
Yes, we'll get it from the devil deeper down.

Now, our engine's built in Glasgow by a very canny Scot,
And he marked it twenty horse-power, but he don't know what is
  what:
When Canadian Bill is firing with the sun-dried gidgee logs,
She can equal thirty horses and a score or so of dogs.
   Sinking down, deeper down,
   Oh, we're going deeper down:
If we fail to get the water, then it's ruin to the squatter,
For the drought is on the station and the weather's growing hotter,
But we're bound to get the water deeper down.

But the shaft has started caving and the sinking's very slow,
And the yellow rods are bending in the water down below,
And the tubes are always jamming and they can't be made to shift
Till we nearly burst the engine with a forty horse-power lift.
   Sinking down, deeper down,
   Oh, we're going deeper down:
Though the shaft is always caving, and the tubes are always jamming,
Yet we'll fight our way to water while the stubborn drill is ramming—
While the stubborn drill is ramming deeper down.

But there's no artesian water, though we've passed three thousand
  feet,
And the contract price is growing, and the boss is nearly beat.
But it must be down beneath us, and it's down we've got to go,
Though she's bumping on the solid rock four thousand feet below.
   Sinking down, deeper down,
   Oh, we're going deeper down:
And it's time they heard us knocking on the roof of Satan's dwellin';
But we'll get artesian water if we cave the roof of hell in—
Oh! we'll get artesian water deeper down.

But it's hark! the whistle's blowing with a wild, exultant blast,
And the boys are madly cheering, for they've struck the flow at
    last;
And it's rushing up the tubing from four thousand feet below,
Till it spouts above the casing in a million-gallon flow.
         And it's down, deeper down—
         Oh, it comes from deeper down;
It is flowing, ever flowing, in a free, unstinted measure
From the silent hidden places where the old earth hides her treasure—
Where the old earth hides her treasures deeper down.

And it's clear away the timber, and it's let the water run;
How it glimmers in the shadow, how it flashes in the sun!
By the silent belts of timber, by the miles of blazing plain
It is bringing hope and comfort to the thirsty land again.
         Flowing down, further down;
         It is flowing further down
To the tortured thirsty cattle, bringing gladness in its going;
Through the droughty days of summer it is flowing, ever flowing—
It is flowing, ever flowing, further down.

SONG OF THE ARTESIAN WATER
Oil on canvas board 18in. × 14in. 1974

Johnson's Antidote

Down along the Snakebite River where the overlanders camp,
Where the serpents are in millions, all of the most deadly stamp;
Where the station-cook in terror, nearly every time he bakes,
Mixes up among the doughboys half a dozen poison-snakes;
Where the wily free-selector walks in armour-plated pants,
And defies the stings of scorpions, and the bites of bull-dog ants:
Where the adder and the viper tear each other by the throat—
There it was that William Johnson sought his snake-bite antidote.

Johnson was a free-selector, and his brain went rather queer,
For the constant sight of serpents filled him with a deadly fear;
So he tramped his free-selection, morning, afternoon, and night,
Seeking for some great specific that would cure the serpent's bite
Till King Billy, of the Mooki, chieftain of the flour-bag head,
Told him, "Spos'n snake bite pfeller, pfellar mostly drop down dead;
Spos'n snake bite old goanna, then you watch a while you see
Old goanna cure himself with eating little pfeller tree."
"That's the cure," said William Johnson, "point me out this plant
    sublime."
But King Billy, feeling lazy, said he'd go another time.
Thus it came to pass that Johnson, having got the tale by rote,
Followed every stray goanna seeking for the antidote.

.   .   .   .

Loafing once beside the river, while he thought his heart would
    break,
There he saw a big goanna fight with a tiger-snake.
In and out they rolled and wriggled, bit each other, heart and soul,
Till the valiant old goanna swallowed his opponent whole.
Breathless, Johnson sat and watched him, saw him struggle up the
    bank,
Saw him nibbling at the branches of some bushes, green and rank;
Saw him, happy and contented, lick his lips, as off he crept,
While the bulging of his stomach showed where his opponent slept
Then a cheer of exultation burst aloud from Johnson's throat;
"Luck at last," said he, "I've struck it! 'tis the famous antidote.

JOHNSON'S ANTIDOTE
Oil on canvas board 18in. × 14in. 1974

"Here it is, the Grand Elixir, greatest blessing ever known—
Twenty thousand men in India die each year of snakes alone;
Think of all the foreign nations, negro, chow, and blackamoor,
Saved from sudden expiration by my wondrous snakebite cure.
It will bring me fame and fortune! In the happy days to be
Men of every clime and nation will be round to gaze on me—
Scientific men in thousands, men of mark and men of note,
Rushing down the Mooki River, after Johnson's antidote.
It will cure *delirium tremens* when the patient's eyeballs stare
At imaginary spiders, snakes which really are not there.
When he thinks he sees them wriggle, when he thinks he sees them
    bloat,
It will cure him just to think of Johnson's Snakebite Antidote."

Then he rushed to the museum, found a scientific man—
"Trot me out a deadly serpent, just the deadliest you can;
I intend to let him bite me, all the risk I will endure.
Just to prove the sterling value of my wondrous snakebite cure.
Even though an adder bit me, back to life again I'd float;
Snakes are out of date, I tell you, since I've found the antidote."
Said the scientific person, "If you really want to die,
Go ahead—but, if you're doubtful, let your sheep-dog have a try.
Get a pair of dogs and try it, let the snake give both a nip;
Give your dog the snakebite mixture, let the other fellow rip;
If he dies and yours survives him then it proves the thing is good.
Will you fetch your dog and try it?" Johnson rather thought he
    would.
So he went and fetched his canine, hauled him forward by the throat.
"Stump, old man," says he, "we'll show them we've the genwine
    antidote."

JOHNSON'S ANTIDOTE
Oil on canvas board 16in. × 14in. 1974

Both the dogs were duly loaded with the poison-gland's contents;
Johnson gave his dog the mixture, then sat down to wait events.
"Mark," he said, "in twenty minutes Stump'll be a-rushing round,
While the other wretched creature lies a corpse upon the ground."
But, alas for William Johnson! ere they'd watched a half-hour's spell
Stumpy was as dead as mutton, t'other dog was live and well.
And the scientific person hurried off with utmost speed,
Tested Johnson's drug and found it was a deadly poison-weed;
Half a tumbler killed an emu, half a spoonful killed a goat—
All the snakes on earth were harmless to that awful antidote.
Down along the Mooki River, on the overlanders' camp,
Where the serpents are in millions, all of the most deadly stamp,
Wanders, daily, William Johnson, down among those poisonous
        hordes,
Shooting every stray goanna calls them "black and yaller frauds".
And King Billy, of the Mooki, cadging for the cast-off coat,
Somehow seems to dodge the subject of the snakebite antidote.

Only a Jockey

"Richard Bennison, a jockey, aged fourteen, while riding William Tell in his training, was thrown and killed. The horse is luckily uninjured."—Melbourne Wire.

Out in the grey cheerless chill of the morning light,
  Out on the track where the night shades still lurk,
Ere the first gleam of the sungod's returning light
  Round come the racehorses early at work.

Reefing and pulling and racing so readily,
  Close sit the jockey-boys holding them hard,
"Steady the stallion there—canter him steadily,
  Don't let him gallop so much as a yard."

Fiercely he fights while the others run wide of him,
  Reefs at the bit that would hold him in thrall,
Plunges and bucks till the boy that's astride of him
  Goes to the ground with a terrible fall.

"Stop him there! Block him there! Drive him in carefully,
  Lead him about till he's quiet and cool.
Sound as a bell! though he's blown himself fearfully,
  Now let us pick up this poor little fool.

"Stunned? Oh, by Jove, I'm afraid it's a case with him;
  Ride for the doctor! keep bathing his head!
Send for a cart to go down to our place with him"—
  No use! One long sigh and the little chap's dead.

Only a jockey-boy, foul-mouthed and bad you see,
  Ignorant, heathenish, gone to his rest.
Parson or Presbyter, Pharisee, Sadducee,
  What did you do for him?—bad was the best.

Negroes and foreigners, all have a claim on you;
  Yearly you send your well-advertised hoard,
But the poor jockey-boy—shame on you, shame on you,
  "Feed ye My little ones"—what said the Lord?

Him ye held less than the outer barbarian,
  Left him to die in his ignorant sin;
Have you no principles, humanitarian?
  Have you no precept—"Go gather them in?"

Knew he God's name? In his brutal profanity
   That name was an oath—out of many but one.
What did he get from our famed Christianity?
   Where has his soul—if he had any—gone?

Fourteen years old, and what was he taught of it?
   What did he know of God's infinite Grace?
Draw the dark curtain of shame o'er the thought of it
   Draw the shroud over the jockey-boy's face.

ONLY A JOCKEY
Oil on canvas board 18in. × 14in. 1974

Been There Before

THERE came a stranger to Walgett town,
  To Walgett town when the sun was low,
And he carried a thirst that was worth a crown,
  Yet how to quench it he did not know;
But he thought he might take those yokels down,
The guileless yokels of Walgett town.

They made him a bet in a private bar,
  In a private bar when the talk was high,
And they bet him some pounds no matter how far
  He could pelt a stone, yet he could not shy
A stone right over the river so brown,
The Darling River at Walgett town.

He knew that the river from bank to bank
  Was fifty yards, and he smiled a smile
As he trundled down; but his hopes they sank,
  For there wasn't a stone within fifty mile;
For the saltbush plain and the open down
Produce no quarries in Walgett town.

The yokels laughed at his hopes o'erthrown,
  And he stood awhile like a man in a dream;
Then he out of his pocket he fetched a stone,
  And pelted it over the silent stream—
He'd been there before; he had wandered down
On a previous visit to Walgett town.

BEEN THERE BEFORE
Oil on canvas board 18in. × 14in. 1974

City of Dreadful Thirst

THE stranger came from Narromine and made his little joke;
"They say we folks in Narromine are narrow-minded folk;
But all the smartest men down here are puzzled to define
A kind of new phenomenon that came to Narromine.

"Last summer up in Narromine 'twas gettin' rather warm—
Two hundred in the water-bag, and lookin' like a storm—
We all were in the private bar, the coolest place in town,
When out across the stretch of plain a cloud came rollin' down.

"We don't respect the clouds up there, they fill us with disgust,
They mostly bring a Bogan shower—three raindrops and some dust;
But each man, simultaneous-like, to each man said, 'I think
That cloud suggests it's up to us to have another drink!'

"There's clouds of rain and clouds of dust—we'd heard of them
    before,
And sometimes in the daily press we read of 'clouds of war'.
But—if this ain't the Gospel truth I hope that I may burst—
That cloud that came to Narromine was just a cloud of thirst.

"It wasn't like a common cloud, 'twas more a sort of haze;
It settled down about the street, and stopped for days and days;
And not a drop of dew could fall, and not a sunbeam shine
To pierce that dismal sort of mist that hung on Narromine.

"Oh, Lord! we had a dreadful time beneath that cloud of thirst!
We all chucked-up our daily work and went upon the burst.
The very blacks about the town, that used to cadge for grub,
They made an organized attack and tried to loot the pub.

"We couldn't leave the private bar no matter how we tried;
Shearers and squatters, union-men and blacklegs side by side
Were drinkin' there and dursn't move, for each was sure, he said,
Before he'd get a half-a-mile the thirst would strike him dead!

"We drank until the drink gave out; we searched from room to room,
And round the pub, like drunken ghosts, went howling through
    the gloom.
The shearers found some kerosene and settled down again,
But all the squatter chaps and I, we staggered to the train.

"And once outside the cloud of thirst we felt as right as pie,
But while we stopped about the town we had to drink or die.
I hear today it's safe enough; I'm going back to work
Because they say the cloud of thirst has shifted on to Bourke.

CITY OF DREADFUL THIRST
Oil on hardboard 18in. × 14in. 1974

"But when you see those clouds about—like this one over here—
All white and frothy at the top, just like a pint of beer,
It's time to go and have a drink, for if that cloud should burst
You'd find the drink would all be gone, for that's a cloud of thirst!"

   . . . . . .

We stood the man from Narromine a pint of half-and-half;
He drank it off without a gasp in one tremendous quaff;
"I joined some friends last night," he said, "in what *they* called a
   spree;
But after Narromine 'twas just a holiday to me.

And now beyond the Western Range, where sunset skies are red,
And clouds of dust, and clouds of thirst, go drifting overhead,
The railway-train is taking back, along the Western Line,
That narrow-minded person on his road to Narromine.